Develop
A Player

How to Play the Position of
Outside-half
(No.10)

Disclaimer

The information in this book is meant to supplement, not replace, proper rugby union training. Like any sport involving speed, equipment, balance and environmental factors, playing the sport of rugby poses some inherent risks. The authors and publisher advise readers to take full responsibility for their safety and know their limits. Before practicing the skills described in this book, be sure your equipment is well- maintained and do not take risks beyond your level of experience, aptitude, training or comfort level.

Copyright

Copyright © 2018, David Christopher Miles All rights reserved.

All rights reserved. Apart from any permitted use under AUS copyright law, no part of this publication may be reproduced or transmitted in any form or by any means, electronic or mechanical, including photocopying, recording, or any information, storage or retrieval system, without permission in writing from the publisher or under license from the Author.

Copyright Licensing Agency Limited.

Printed in AUS for Develop A Player by Develop A Player.

ISBN: 978-0-6482535-2-5

Purpose

The purpose of this book is to provide the player, family, coach and player's support network with the information needed for positional excellence in the position of **Outside-half (No. 10)** in rugby union.

Objectives

The objectives of this book are:

- ☑ To provide the reader with an understanding of the natural physical and mental development of young players in the sport of rugby union.
- ☑ To explain the demands of rugby union and use that information to help guide the player's development.
- ☑ To provide a blueprint for the core conditioning needed to achieve results in the game of rugby union.
- ☑ To provide an insight into what selectors and coaches are looking for at a representative level.
- ☑ To provide FREE access to a professional player development portal **www.developaplayer.com** whereby the player can record and share their rugby development with friends, family, coaches, sponsors and selectors.

Table Of Contents

Chapter 1:
Understanding emotional and physical development

Overview

In this chapter you will gain knowledge of the following:

- ☑ **Background**
- ☑ **How an athlete's brain works**
- ☑ **The role of natural testosterone in sports development**

Background

The brain is an amazing thing. An athlete who wants to be the best they can be in a sport they love is equally as amazing. Both need to be understood, nurtured and allowed to develop over time.

By understanding the brain, the player, coach, and supportive family members can help both the brain and the player achieve truly awesome things.

The brain grows like a tub of sprouts left in the sun. Brain cells get longer and make new connections. The left half of the cortex grows slower than the right in all human babies, but in males, it develops over a longer period, with the female hormone oestrogen promoting faster growth in

1

girls than boys. As the right half of the cortex grows, it tries to make connections with the left half. In boys, the left half of the brain isn't ready to make the connection. After reaching out to the left and being unable to plug in, the right half stays where it is.

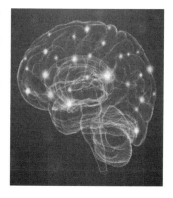

As a result, the right half of a boy's brain is richer in internal connections but poorer in cross connections to the other half of the brain. It is therefore clear that regular practice actually helps the brain's connections to connect permanently, so encouragement and teaching affect the shape and power of the brain in later life. So why is this important to know?

How the rugby brain works

Our brains are brilliant and flexible devices that are always learning. Parents normally teach a young boy how to avoid getting into fights and how to solve disputes peacefully, reinforcing that knocking someone over is not tolerated.

Coaches, who aren't aware of the brain's development, ask these same young developing players to forget all those early social rules, so delicately taught, and demand that they go out onto the field of play and be a dynamic and unstoppable rugby sensation.

Some boys are ready for this challenge and take to it like a duck to water, however to other this can be challenging and therefore need a little more time, and a little more nurturing from their parents and coaches before they are ready to compete to the fullest of their ability.

At these early stages of a young man's rugby career we can normally identify four types of rugby players.

- Type 1 – The "Thinker" who eats, breathes and sleeps rugby.
- Type 2 – The "Bulldozer" who loves the physical game.
- Type 3 – The "Star" who is expected to be playing rugby.
- Type 4 – The "Developing" kid who is not yet sure why he is playing rugby.

The role of natural testosterone in sports development

Testosterone in varying degrees affects every boy. It gives a boy growth spurts, makes him want to be active, and makes him competitive.

Testosterone triggers significant changes:

- Around the age of 4 – Initial activity and boyishness.

- Around the age of 12 – In rapid growth and disorientation.
- Around the age of 14 – Is testing limits and breaking through to early manhood.

The boy with testosterone in his bloodstream likes to know who the boss is, but also wants to be treated fairly. Bad environments bring out the worst in him. The boy with lots of testosterone needs strong guidance and a safe, ordered environment to help him develop his rugby ability and leadership is needed to channel his rugby enthusiasm productively.

Boys need to learn empathy and feeling, and be shown tenderness if they are to progress in life's journey. As the rugby player develops he does not need ridicule and blame from his parents or coach. It is important that these role models provide understanding and support. It is our job to honour and steer a young man in a healthy direction if he is to become a well-rounded rugby player for the future.

There is hope for all the four types of rugby players as natural windows of accelerated developmental exist which the player, parent and coach should be mindful of and be ready to take fully advantage of in the pursuit of sporting excellence. Chapter 8 takes a look at these developmental windows in greater detail

Chapter 2:
The four disciplines of great rugby

Overview

In this chapter you will gain knowledge of the following:

- ☑ **Attacking rugby**
- ☑ **Defensive rugby**
- ☑ **Physical conditioning**
- ☑ **Mental conditioning**
- ☑ **The influencers on the four disciplines**

Background

In the modern era of rugby union, there is considerable emphasis put on size, strength, genetic make-up and aggression. This emphasis is detrimental to the young player.

It is true that at the highest level of professional rugby and international competition, size does matter. Gone are the days when front row players had a certain shape, second row players were the tallest on the field and wingers were speedsters with little or nothing in the way of bulk muscle.

That being said, there are exceptions to size. If we look deeper than just the physical appearance we can see the journey these players have been on which led them to become the top players in their current positions.

Rugby union is seen by many as a complicated game of massive collisions, infringements, stoppages and periods of no action. Others see the sport as a strategic movement of players in complex formations achieving superiority in numbers in certain regions of the pitch, which leads to scoring opportunities. Both perspectives can be true, but there are a multitude of additional interpretations in-between.

We need to help young players entering the game of rugby union understand that the game is actually one to be enjoyed. We need to help them understand it is a game of strategy, evasion and the core disciplines of attack and defence, but also of physical and mental conditioning. If the young athletes can understand these aspects and execute them with pace, power, agility and skill, then irrespective of their size, strength or genetic make-up, they can compete at the highest level of rugby union and reap the emotional and social benefits of success.

Attacking rugby

Attacking rugby can be broken down into two scenarios; when you have the ball in your possession and when you don't.

Attacking with the ball in possession

When you have the ball in your possession you have the advantage. Sometimes young players' forget that and start to panic, which leads to mistakes in running, passing and catching.

If you are attacking with the ball, then the opposition needs to react and try to stop you. If you can attack quicker, with greater skill and more purpose, the outcome will be positive.

The ability to attack with confidence stems from three simple building blocks:

- Attack space (knowledge).
- Know you can execute a skill with confidence and precision (practice).
- Keep focused and be in the moment (commitment).

Attacking without the ball in possession

Due to the fluidity of the game, the conditioning, and the number of players on the field, the support role of team members in attack is equally as essential as the primary attacking player himself.

In younger age groups, if a player breaks through a tackle line they tend to run the length of the playing area and score. However, as the size of the playing area and the number of players on the field increases, the defence tends to regroup, meaning that attacking without the ball in possession is equally as important.

The ability to attack without the ball in position, therefore, comes down to three key aspects:

- Anticipating where the likely contact point with the defence will be and be in position to keep the attacking movement going (support).
- Providing options for attacking continuity (understanding).
- Decide what the best role will be in providing those support options for attacking continuity (be a team player).

Defensive rugby

Defensive play has evolved dramatically in recent times, primarily down to the influence of other sports. Defensive structures, defensive roles, and defensive policies have all played a major part in the modern game of rugby union, leading to more strategic thought on how to break down those defensive patterns.

It is important to also understand where attacking sides are most likely to score, and then develop a defensive policy in response, but not at the expense of the natural skills and flair of players being able to defend instinctively.

To understand how and when to defend effectively statistical analysis is very important. If we look at the 2014 statistics information from the southern hemisphere Super 16 sides where tries were scored some interesting insights can be drawn.

Team	From own lineout	From own scrum	From restart receipts	From open play - tap	From kick receipts	From turnovers
Blues	23	13	12	4	28	19
Brumbies	25	6	15	1	34	19
Bulls	23	9	12	2	33	21
Cheetahs	22	5	12	5	34	22
Chiefs	18	12	13	4	29	24
Crusaders	20	10	14	2	36	18
Highlanders	18	11	13	3	33	22
Hurricanes	16	11	14	3	33	23
Lions	25	10	13	3	26	22
Rebels	21	13	13	4	31	19
Reds	24	12	10	3	29	23
Sharks	21	9	13	2	36	20
Stormers	22	11	10	2	33	20
Waratahs	19	13	15	4	27	23
W-Force	22	12	10	3	33	21

Average	21	10	13	3	32	21

From reviewing this kind of data we can start to identify insights on what to defend and why thereby providing a competitive edge over the opposition. For example, if we were to use the above data to develop our defensive policy we could conclude that if a team was to defend well from kick receipts, lineouts and turnovers, then they would have statistically reduced the attacking sides' probability of scoring by 74%.

We can, therefore, look at defence principles associated with set pieces and broken play to become more effective in this part of the game.

Defending set pieces

Set pieces are defined as either lineouts or scrums. Based on the statistics identified above, we would break each down into the elements and put in place defensive practices that would focus on the following:

- **Lineout Defence** – Look to defend the following areas:
  - o At the point of catch in the lineout.
  - o On the short side of the lineout (between the touch line and the 5M line).
  - o On the immediate open side of the lineout (between the 15m line and the goal posts).

- o On the far open side (between the goal posts and the opposite touch line).
- **Scrum Defence** – Look to defend the following areas:
  - o Defend the scrum by not retreating.
  - o Within 2m of the scrum (both sides).
  - o Within 15m of the scrum (both sides).

By looking at these specific aspects of set piece play we are identifying defensive channels. By understanding these channels, defensive patterns can be developed and adapted to counter sides that are more likely to attack from set pieces.

Defending broken play

Broken play defence is defined as either defending from when the ball has been kicked to the attacking team, or when the attacking team has maintained possession after a contact situation. By using the playing statistics identified earlier we would again look at defensive policies around the following:

- **Restart Receipts** – Look to defend the following areas:
  - o Within 10m of the attacker receiving the ball (to prevent momentum).
  - o Behind the first defensive line (in case of a line break).

- o Deep (in case of chips, grubbers and territory advantage).
- **Tap** – Look to defend the following areas:
  - o Within 10m of the attacker receiving the ball (to prevent momentum).
  - o Within 15m of the tap (to prevent early line breaks).
- **Kick Receipts** – Look to defend the following areas:
  - o Within 10m of the attacker receiving the ball (to prevent momentum).
  - o Behind the first defensive line (in case of a line break).
  - o Deep (in case of chips, grubbers and territory advantage).
- **Turnovers** – Look to defend the following areas:
  - o Within 1m of the turnover (to counter pick and go).
  - o Within 3m of the turnover (to counter first receiver).
  - o Within 5m of the turnover (to counter first receiver running onto the ball at pace).

Physical conditioning

Young rugby union players should find enjoyment in the game and be able to compete, and therefor a certain level of base conditioning is a very important factor that allows them to do so.

A typical length of a rugby field is 100m for the field of play plus the depth of the in-goal areas at both ends of the field, say 10m each - total 120m. The width is typically 70m so the area = 120m x 70m = 8400 sq m. A full size pitch (22m in-goal) would be 144m x 70m = 10080 sq m

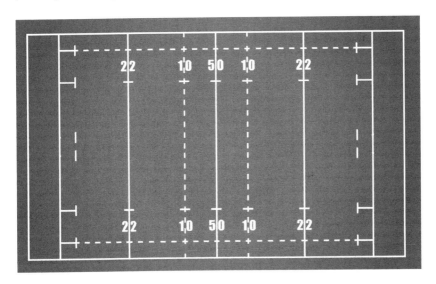

Being able to run is essential. Rugby, after all, rugby is an active game, and to be able to enjoy the game, the young athlete must have a sufficient base level of physical conditioning to be able to compete for the duration of each match.

- **Under 6s':**
  - ○ Field size = 50m x 25m
  - ○ Playing time = 10 minute haves
  - ○ Playing numbers = 7 per side
- **Under 7s':**
  - ○ Field size = 50m x 25m
  - ○ Playing time = 15 minute haves
  - ○ Playing numbers = 7 per side
- **Under 8s' and U9s':**
  - ○ Field size = 70m x 35m (half field)
  - ○ Playing time = 15 minute haves (20 minutes for U9s'
  - ○ Playing numbers = 7 per side (10 per side for U9s')
- **Under 10s' and 11s':**
  - ○ Field size = 120m x 65m
  - ○ Playing time = 20 minute haves
  - ○ Playing numbers = 12 per side
- **Under 12s':**
  - ○ Field size = 120m x 70m
  - ○ Playing time = 25 minute haves
  - ○ Playing numbers = 15 per side
- **Under 13's to Under 19s':**
  - ○ Field size = 120m x 70m
  - ○ Playing time = 35 minute haves
  - ○ Playing numbers = 15 per side

When considering the dynamics and body movements of a rugby player, it is interesting to know that the average distance a forward runs with the ball in hand during a game is between 5 to 10 meters in any one carry and that a back normally runs on average between 10 to 30 meters. That doesn't seem like a lot and, in fact, it isn't when compared to athletics where kids run hundreds, if not thousands of meters in a single athletic race.

Rugby union, however, is unique in that it requires forwards and backs to perform those relatively short distances when the ball is in hand at 100% output, reload, and then go again. Additionally, the sport requires the player to be operating at 60-70% of their maximum in support and then be able to immediately reach that 100% output the moment they have the ball in hand.

By understanding these dynamics, we can put in place the necessary conditioning that will help rugby athletes have the physical stamina necessary to perform in these attack and defence scenarios.

General Physical conditioning

To get an idea of the general physical conditioning levels needed to perform in a particular playing position at a particular age, the Develop A Player organization has mapped out a number of range parameters as a guide aligned to two commonly used tests which are further explained in Chapter 3. Additional, and specific physical conditioning for different playing positions is outlined in Chapter 4, which provides a deeper understanding of the conditioning needed for great rugby.

- Recommended conditioning test 1 - Multi-stage Fitness Test (Bleep Test) for aerobic endurance.
- Recommended conditioning test 2 - 30m Sprint Fatigue Power Maintenance Test for speed and power.

Mental conditioning

Sports play a huge role in our society, and as such mental conditioning needs to be taken seriously as it can play a huge role in helping athletes achieve success. Participation in childhood sports can be a rewarding experience and a good introduction can lead to a lifetime of enjoyment.

For parents, coaches and support networks, understanding who understand mental development in young players can increase the player's overall involvement and enjoyment of sports. As the adults guiding children in sports, it is important for them to remember that, while there are some fundamental building blocks for success, no two people are completely alike.

Understanding a child's development helps adults avoid unnecessary frustration and inappropriate expectations while simultaneously creating an environment of learning, increased participation, and fun.

Young children (ages 7-10 years) face two major challenges in sports:

- Learning how to get along with friends.
- Learning how to interact with authority figures other than their   parents.

At this young age, learning to cooperate within a team and compromising for the interests of someone else are major accomplishments. Children at this young stage of a sport are just beginning to develop the ability to see the world from the perspective of others. Parents and coaches should make a clear distinction between what is acceptable behavior and what is not. Since the child is learning, we need to provide them with the opportunity to grow through guided trial and error. It is important to remember that fun, exploration, and developing a love of sports are key elements at this age. If competition and winning become the main themes, these are most likely fostered by adults, which means they should temper their competitive nature in the interests of the child.

Pre-adolescents (ages 10-13 years) face the social challenges of developing best friends and gaining acceptance from peers. Social relationships are one of the developmental milestones that this age group is navigating. They want to be part of a group and often fear being embarrassed. Developing a same-sex best friend is a major task of this social stage. Pre-teens tend to be loyal to their friends and make many decisions based on maintaining their friendships. "Sports hopping" is an example of a decision based on maintaining a friendship. Sports hopping occurs when a pre-teen changes sports or quits participating in sports because of friendships.

During the pre-teen phase of development, practices should be structured that allow for social interactions. Coaches often view social interactions at practices as 'goof off' time. Contrary to many coaches' beliefs, a practice which contains structured social interaction as part of a regular routine helps develop team relationships.

Adolescents (ages 14-18 years) face the developmental challenge of defining who they are and how they fit into the world. Identity development is a complex process that involves applying the training and teaching we have given them, while the teen is trying on different identities. The teen is attempting to discover who they are and clarify their values through exploring different facets of their personality. This process occurs as parents and coaches wring their hands and watch as their own hair turns gray in exasperation!

Often, we see the teen's identity search in the clothes they wear, the music they listen to, and the changes they make in who their peers are. Being tolerant of the adolescent while they try out new ideas is an important behavior for parents and coaches. Tolerance for new behaviors is guided by the rules that the behaviors do not place the teen in danger or interfere with team rules and goals. The second major transition during the teenage phase is recognizing that sports is truly important in life.

The teen makes the transition in identity from 'I play rugby' to 'I am a rugby player.' Participation in sports and being an athlete becomes a significant piece of their identity. Helping the teenage athlete enhance the technical mastery of their chosen sport while supporting their growth as an individual, is a challenge facing both parents and coaches.

Regardless of an athlete's age, there are several common themes that relate to participation in the sport that should be considered;

- To have fun
- For fitness
- Being with friends
- To compete

The social aspect of sports and having fun is appealing to the young athlete. Competition or winning is not the predominant motivator.

Recognizing the young athlete's need for encouragement, socialization, and fun is paramount. If the young athlete develops a love of sports, then with support and a healthy coaching environment, the drive for competition and mastery naturally develops.

No matter the age of your young athlete, there are several simple keys that help sports participation and competition evolve naturally:

- Be supportive.
- Avoid TMTS (Too Much Too Soon); children's natural drive for competition will evolve as they age.
- Structure time to include social interaction and fun.
- Help your teen incorporate athletics as part of their identity by being positive.

The influencers on the four disciplines

Fathers, mothers & care givers

Sports should be fun for kids. Treat sport as a game, it is not a business for kids.

With all the money in professional sports today, it is hard for parents to understand that it is just good fun to young athletes. The primary goal should be to have fun and enjoy the healthy competition.

Young athletes' compete in sports for many reasons. They enjoy the competition, like the social aspect, engage with being part of a team, and enjoy the challenge of setting goals. Parents and coaches may have a different agenda than your young athlete, and as such they need to recognise that it is their sport, and not that of the parent or coach.

Emphasize a mental focus on the process of execution instead of results or trophies. We live in a society that focuses on results and winning, but winning comes from working the process and enjoying the results. Teach your young athlete to focus on the process of the challenge of playing one shot, one tackle, or one run at a time instead of the number of wins or trophies.

Parents and coaches are role models for young athletes'. As such, you should model composure and poise on the sidelines. When you are at a competition, your young athlete will mimic your behavior as well as other role models. You become a role model in how you react to a close race or the questionable behavior of a competitor or official. Stay calm, composed, and in control during games so your young athlete can mimic those positive behaviors.

What are some of the things parents can do to help their kids enjoy and succeed at sports?

5 Rules for supportive parents and care givers

1. Do what you can to make sure your child is having a positive experience with coaches and teammates. The wrong coach can turn a kid off to a sport. Similarly, conflicts with teammates and peer pressure can make sports quite unpleasant. Help your child work out these interpersonal issues. In some instances, you may need to intervene or intercede on his behalf.

2. Try to determine if your child seems better suited for team sports or for individual sports. Some kids love the camaraderie of team sports. Others enjoy competing on their own. And of course, some kids like both.

3. Be sure to model good sportsmanship, grace, gentleness, and integrity on and off the athletic field. If you behave inappropriately at training and matches, your children are likely to do the same.

4. Lots of kids have difficulty managing busy schedules, which include games, practices, travel, family activities and school work. In many instances, the parents and their kids are spread quite thin and can easily become overwhelmed. Help your child find a balance and make sure they

do not have too much on their plates at any one time.

5. Be aware of burn out. If your child has lost some of their enthusiasm and their performance has declined, your youngster may be burnt out. Talk with them to see if they need a break, a new challenge, or a different approach to their sport.

Coaches

Take the time to reflect on why it is you coach. This is beneficial not only for personal growth but also in creating an awareness of changes in our motivation.

- Motivation (why we do what we do) affects our behaviour (what it is we do).

Therefore, changes in our motivation can be reflected in our behaviours and also in our wellbeing.

Research suggests that coaching for intrinsic reasons such as love, joy and passion is associated with better outcomes. These outcomes include the health and wellbeing of the coach, improved coach-athlete relationships, athlete motivation, satisfaction, and performance.

Three psychological needs have been identified as important in fostering greater intrinsic motivation for an activity. To what degree do you feel these needs are satisfied by your coaching work?

- The need for autonomy (the desire to feel that your actions emanate from your own choice).
- The need for competence (the desire to be good at the activity).
- The need for relatedness (the desire to be connected to others).

Those who feel they coach because they want to, are good at it. Coaching allows them to continue relationships within their sport and with their athletes, display more intrinsic motivation for coaching, and coach with a more autonomy-supportive style.

Therefore, being aware of why you coach your sport is an important and reflective practice.

Your coaching motivation plays a crucial role in the facilitation of a healthy coaching environment, both physically and psychologically. Working in an environment that supports your needs will help you get the best out of yourself as well as your athletes.

Sports coaches assist athletes in developing to their full potential. They are responsible for training athletes in a sport by analyzing their performances, instructing in relevant skills, and by providing encouragement. But you are also responsible for the guidance of the athlete in life and in their chosen sport.

Consequently, the roles of the coach will be many and varied, and range from instructor, assessor, friend, mentor, facilitator, chauffeur, demonstrator, adviser, supporter, fact finder, motivator, counselor, organizer, planner, and even the fountain of all knowledge.

In relation to sports, the role of the coach is to create the right conditions for learning and to find ways of motivating the athletes. For athletes who are already highly motivated, the task is to maintain that motivation and generate excitement and enthusiasm.

The coach will need to be able to: assist athletes in preparing training programs, communicate effectively with athletes, assist athletes in developing new skills and use evaluation tests to monitor training progress and predict performance.

The role of the coach can be seen as a very difficult task requiring a very special person, and therefore, they need to be ready to perform in this role.

Chapter 3:
General conditioning for the modern game

Overview

In this chapter you will gain knowledge of the following:

- ☑ **The science behind rugby conditioning**
- ☑ **Conditioning tests and performance ranges**

Background

There are different thoughts on how to undertake the right conditioning for young players and there are loads of online resources that can be used to undertake the conditioning evaluation.

In this chapter the most useful tests relevant to young players has been identified, how to undertake those tests and what the expected performance ranges per age group should be.

Firstly, this book does not recommend any weight training for young players in any rugby position until about 15 years of age, as the muscles, tendons, and bones are still growing and require careful management if the player is to enjoy later years of development and injury-free playing.

The recommended baseline tests are to assess aerobic endurance, power, and speed.

26

The science behind rugby conditioning

As a child grows, his nervous system becomes more mature. With this maturity, the child becomes more and more capable of performing increasingly complex actions. The rate at which these motor skills emerge is sometimes a worry for parents. Caregivers frequently fret about whether or not their children are developing these skills at a normal rate. As mentioned above, rates may vary somewhat, however, nearly all children begin to exhibit these motor skills at a fairly consistent rate unless some type of disability is present.

There are two types of motor skills:

- **Gross** (or large) motor skills involve the larger muscles including the arms and legs. Actions requiring gross motor skills include walking, running, balance and coordination. When evaluating gross motor skills, the factors that experts look at include strength, muscle tone, movement quality and the range of movement.

- **Fine** (or small) motor skills involve the smaller muscles in the fingers, toes, eyes and other areas. The actions that require fine motor skills tend to be more intricate, such as drawing, writing, grasping objects, throwing, waving and catching.

Physical development in children follows a directional pattern:

- **Large muscles** - develop before small muscles. Muscles in the body's core, legs and arms develop before those in the fingers and hands. Children learn how to perform gross (or large) motor skills such as walking before they learn to perform fine (or small) motor skills such as drawing.
- **The center** - of the body develops before the outer regions. Muscles located at the core of the body become stronger and develop sooner than those in the feet and hands.

Conditional tests and performance ranges

There are many conditioning tests available to coaches and selectors to evaluate a player's current and future suitability in a sport, or indeed, to a particular position either at the representative or elite level.

Some prefer a series of detailed evaluations taking metrics of: speed and quickness, strength and power, agility and flexibility, and some prefer the more simple approach of taking a player's height and weight at a certain age and then using the parents height and weight as an indication of what the young athlete will attain once fully matured.

Some of the main tests used are identified below with the recommended two highlighted:

Fitness Component	Evaluation Test
Anaerobic Endurance	Running-based Anaerobic Sprint Test
Aerobic Endurance	Multistage Fitness Test or Bleep test - **Recommended**
Agility	Illinois agility run test
Balance	Standing Stork Test Blind
Body Composition	Body Fat Percentage
Coordination	Hand Eye coordination
Fitness General	Wilf Paish Rugby Football Tests
Flexibility	Sit and Reach test
Psychology	Sport Competition Anxiety Test
Reaction Time	Ruler Drop Test
Strength - Core	Core muscle strength and stability test
Strength - Elastic	Standing Long Jump test
Strength - General	Burpee Test
Speed and Power	30 M Sprint Fatigue Power Maintenance Test - **Recommended**
Aerobic Endurance	Yo-Yo (Stage 1) and Yo-Yo (Stage 2)
Aerobic Endurance	300M endurance run

Recommended baseline test 1 for aerobic endurance

Multistage Fitness Test (Bleep Test) - The Multistage Fitness Test, more commonly known as the Bleep Test has been around for many years and, as such, good data exists to draw comparisons from.

How to run baseline test 1

This test requires the athlete to run 20m in time with a beep from a CD recording. The athlete must place one foot on or beyond the 20m marker at the end of each shuttle.

- When signaled by the CD the athlete runs from cone C to cone B.
- The athlete continues running between the cones as signaled by the CD.
- The assistant keeps a record of each completed lap .
- A warning is given when the athlete does not complete a successful out and back shuttle (cone B to C and back to B) in the allocated time, the next time the athlete does not complete a successful shuttle the test is stopped.

- The assistant records the total distance completed.

The below is a table broken down by age and performance level for the bleep test:

Age	Excellent	Above Average	Average	Below Average	Poor
6 - 8	N/a	N/a	N/a	N/a	N/a
8 - 10	N/a	N/a	N/a	N/a	N/a
10 - 12	L8 S9	L7 S1	L6 S6	L6 S1	< L5 S3
12 - 14	L11 S2	L8 S9	L7 S1	L6 S6	< L6 S1
14 - 16	L12 S7	L11 S2	L8 S9	L7 S1	< L6 S6
17 - 20	L12 S12	L11 S6	L9 S2	L7 S6	< L7 S3
21 - 30	L12 S12	L11 S7	L9 S3	L7 S8	< L7 S5
31 - 40	L11 S7	L10 S4	L6 S10	L6 S7	< L6 S4
41 - 50	L10 S4	L9 S4	L6 S9	L5 S9	< L5 S2

Recommended baseline test 2 for speed and power

30m Sprint Fatigue Power Maintenance Test requires the athlete to complete 10 x 30m sprints.

How to run baseline test 2

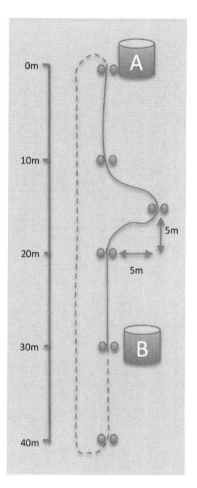

- The athlete warms up for 10 minutes.
- The assistant sets up the course as per the diagram opposite using the cones.
- The assistant gives the command "GO" and starts the stopwatch.
- The athlete sprints from A to B between the cones deviating 5m sideways in the middle of the sprint.
- The assistant stops the stopwatch when the athlete's torso crosses the finish line at B and records the time.
- The athlete jogs slowly back to point A (taking

no longer than 30 seconds to do so) following the route on the diagram.

- The athlete is to complete a total of 10 sprints from A to B and the assistant is to record the times.
- Determine the average speed of the first three trials and divide it by the average speed of the last three trials.

Calculation Example

- 1st Set of 3 = 7.1s, 6.9s, 6.9s;
- 2nd Set of 4 = 7.0s, 7.2s, 7.1s, 7.3s;
- 3rd Set of 3 = 7.3s, 7.4s, 7.5s

The average of the first 3 times (7.1s, 6.9s, 6.9s) = 6.97s and the average of the last 3 times (7.3s, 7.4s, 7.5s) = 7.4s

Power Maintenance = 6.97s / 7.4s = 0.94

The table below is broken down by age and performance level for the Sprint Fatigue Power Maintenance Test:

Age	Excellent	Above Average	Average	Below Average	Poor
6 - 8	N/a	N/a	N/a	N/a	N/a
8 - 10	N/a	N/a	N/a	N/a	N/a
10 - 12	>89%	85-89%	80-84%	75-79%	<75%
12 - 14	>89%	85-89%	80-84%	75-79%	<75%
14 - 16	>89%	85-89%	80-84%	75-79%	<75%
17 - 20	>89%	85-89%	80-84%	75-79%	<75%
21 - 30	>89%	85-89%	80-84%	75-79%	<75%
31 - 40	>89%	85-89%	80-84%	75-79%	<75%
41 - 50	N/a	N/a	N/a	N/a	N/a

Chapter 4:
How to play the position of Outside-half
(No. 10)

Overview

In this chapter you will gain knowledge of the following:

- ☑ **The Outside-half's role in the back line**
- ☑ **Passing essentials for the Outside-half**
- ☑ **Kicking essentials for the Outside-half**
- ☑ **Outside-half's role at set piece and open play**
- ☑ **Role in defensive shapes and structures**
- ☑ **Role in controlling different game scenarios**

Background

The Outside-half is often considered the go-to man on the field. The person in this position controls the attack and dictates how a team decides to penetrate an opposition's defence. The Outside-half is often used as the vital orchestrator of a defensive system. Their primary job in defence is to produce the line speed of a defensive line to cut down space from the opposition, in turn forcing the attack to execute under pressure.

The role of a Outside-half varies from team to team. However, a good Outside-half who inspires to excel in their position will have a substantial skill set and can produce high-level skills under pressure. An Outside-half should be continually looking to make ground and identify weaknesses in an opposition's defence. A great Outside-half can locate the space in the defence and consistently make the best decisions on how to exploit the shortcomings of the opposition. Team strategy and game plans are often executed through the Outside-half who plays a pivotal role in adapting to the game as it unfolds as well as in initiating patterns and plays from the set piece.

This position requires the highest degree of talent in the execution of skills such as game management, leadership, distribution, and kicking.

Passing essentials for the Outside-half

Passing is an essential part of the game of Rugby, and none should be better at it than the Outside-half. There are a variety of passing types, however, each of them has six essential core elements:

1. Correct hand position on the ball.
2. Proper body position concerning the direction of the pass.
3. Exact head position to the direction of the pass.
4. Follow through with the hands.

5. Apply force and direction.

Breaking these skills down in detail, the Outside-half must be able to pass with a variety of passes under pressure effectively. They must be able to pass left/right in a single movement with no back swing.

In the modern game, the Outside-half must be able to deliver a spiral pass (the reason this pass is used is to clear the ball from a congested area to a less crowded area at speed). This pass travels greater distances at speed. Frequently used at most rucks / tackle / scrum / lineouts.

Kicking essentials for the Outside-half

As the game of rugby develops, so does the need to be comfortable in all aspects of the game. There are only three reasons why kicking should take place on a rugby field; to restart play, to gain territory or to score a try.

In the modern game we see teams kicking from all areas of the field as they try to exploit the space left by defenders. Gone are the days of only kicking for territory. The modern Outside-half must, therefore, be able to master six basic types of kicks:

1. The distance kick
2. The cross-field kick
3. The grubber

4. The chip
5. The conversion
6. Other kicks

The distance kick

For an Outside-half, it is crucial that they can execute a competent end-over-end kick. This kick is often used to gain territory, especially when trying to relieve pressure from deep within their half. It is also the most effective kick when aiming to catch the opposition off guard with a cross-field kick. The basics of the kick are simple. The ball is caught and held with an excellent "W" position.

The non-kicking foot is grounded, the kicking leg strikes the ball on the point of the ball, and a high follow-through should follow. Head stays down over the ball as arms lift and finishes in a position in line with where the ball has landed. A player should ensure they kick the ball with the laces of their boots (the middle of the foot).

The cross-field kick

The cross-field kick is a great attacking option for an Outside-half. This kick requires plenty of communication and pinpoint accuracy. The kick is often best performed while on the move. The catch is crucial, and to get the ball where they want it to go with the kick, the player must ensure their hips are in line with where they want the ball to end up. Alignment of the hips to where the ball should land is an essential part of properly executing the kick.

As an Outside-half, you want to be able to put enough flight and height on the ball to enable your outside backs to compete. The better cross-field kicks ensure the ball is in front of your players, so they are running onto it, this gives your team an advantage over defenders as they are on the front foot. They run with purpose and can perform a jump from a running start, not a static position which a defender may find themselves in.

The grubber kick

The grubber is a highly efficient kick for many reasons. It can be used when under pressure, and to turn the opposition's defence. It is also a great tactic to use when wishing to manage the time left in the game.

Often a team will drill the ball into touch to form a set piece and re-organise their defensive system. It is also used in attacking situations to score tries and fly hack the ball when it is loose on the ground.

The key to executing an effective grubber is the angle of the ball when it is kicked.

The chip kick

The chip is a highly effective kick for an outside-half to execute. Often a defensive back three will set up deep in defence, meaning a distance kick is hard to accomplish. The chip kick can be performed to get over the gain line. Often, if this kick is efficiently executed, a defensive team will bring their back three up in the hope it will prevent an Outside-half from continuing to implement it.

The chip is also a great way of attacking against a blitz defence or in a one-on-one situation. To perform this kick effectively, you will execute it on the move. The chip kick is a harder kick as you have to catch, kick, run and collect all in a matter of seconds. The best way to perfect this kick is to practice against a pressured defence. The kick is again performed with the middle of the foot. Ensure the release of the ball is below knee height, which allows power to be pushed into the ball. Whether an Outside-half kicks from front on or sideways depends on the situation, but having enough flight to regain or contest possession is crucial to this kick.

The conversion

At higher levels of play, coaches look at conversion success rate when recruiting players. In the modern day, you see an array of kicking styles and stances. Firstly the non-kicking leg should be grounded next to the ball on the tee with your eyes and head firmly looking at the ball.

As you kick, ensure you do so with the middle of the foot for a strong follow through. A good practice drill is to stand on the try line facing the rugby sticks. Of course, you can only see the one on the side you are on.

From here practice kicking the ball off the tee, this will help work on your accuracy. The power will develop with technique, age, and specific training.

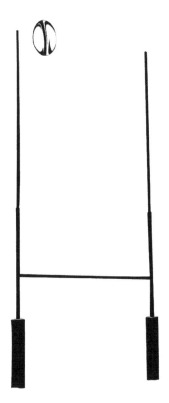

Other kicks

- **The drop kick** - Not only is this style of kick a way of restarting play, but it is also an opportunity to score points. The Outside-half is often tasked with restarting the game as they can dictate where they want the ball to go as well as organise a defensive line from there. So kicking the ball into the right areas is crucial for strategic point scoring and tactical territory gains.

- **A restart from the half way line** - Usually, you will try to aim as close as possible to the touchlines ensuring the ball travels 10 meters. This gives your team a chance to compete for the ball. Alternatively, you will kick deep and organise a strong kick chase. This ensures a team has to play from deep within their half or kick for territory. As a key attacking threat, the Outside-half will often dictate how the team plays.

- **A restart from the 22-meter line** - Usually, you will try to aim as close as possible to the touchlines, however, the ball only has to cross the 22-meter line. The Outside-half has the option to kick short in an attempt to regain the ball or kick deep and organise a strong kick chase.

Outside-half's role at set piece and open play

.

The Outside-half's role in the attack is to fundamentally find space in the defence and ensure the attacking team is gaining territory. This can be done by passing, running or kicking.

An Outside-half is predominantly going to stand deep in the attacking line and should ensure they are coming onto the pass at speed. By starting in this manner, they provide the attacking line momentum, and the defence has to make a decision.

The Outside-half should always be thinking whether the right option is to pass to a teammate, or run into space. An Outside-half can attract defenders by the run they make and then look for a late pass into space. The Outside-half should also take note of the body position of a defender. If their hips are turned (not square to the attacker) this means the defender is in a weak stance and should be exploited in the attack.

By targeting this defender, space should open up, and a Outside-half can run through or ensure a pass finds a teammate that is running a support line.

As the Outside-half develops, they should be more aware of the link play and support moves that attract defenders and open up space. Miss passes, dummies, switches and wrap plays are all moves that can be done on the gain line to commit a defender to tackle. The Outside-half can spot a mismatch in defence, and as long as their pass is the correct one, the attacking team can execute a move that penetrates the defensive line.

Running from depth

As briefly mentioned before, the attacking structure of a team will be able to penetrate defences more efficiently by running from depth. An Outside-half should be running onto the ball when receiving a pass. By doing so, they are engaging defenders and drawing them into making a tackle. In turn, this allows holes in the defences to become more extensive as defenders are making decisions of whether to hold their line or move on to another attacker.

The line of run from the Outside-half will dictate how many defenders are attracted. By using footwork and ball movement, a defender has to make a decision. A good Outside-half will be able to access the situation and exploit the defender's decision. By running from depth, the other attacking players are also able to come onto the ball with pace and power. It will give the team a chance to spot holes in the defence and hit a good line.

Open play

Open play attack is a great way to score tries. Free flowing instinctive rugby is what all great teams aspire towards. An Outside-half's direction and inherent nature are crucial to getting an attacking team operating at its full potential.

An Outside-half should always be an option from the ruck, whether it is from the first point of contact as the first receiver, or the alternative option of standing behind a forward runner. This gives the attacking side more time to execute a penetrative move as they have more depth to work with which gives you time to make good decisions. Open play attack can still involve structure. The Outside-half will decide whether a team attacks through the forwards or backs, whether a team plays wide or tight, or whether a kick option may be more beneficial.

Flair

Flair refers to being able to do something special or instinctive. A good Outside-half oozes talent. Think about the excellent Outside-halves you watched growing up. What did they all have in common? They could create something out of nothing. An Outside-half should be allowed to express themselves and show off their talents in the right situation.

Would a chip and chase on your 5m line be a good option? If you score from it, you may argue yes. However, I believe the best Outside-halves who possess this flair attribute are those that let it shine at the right time.

An Outside-half is brave in decision making and doesn't second guess their decisions. If you do something, put 100% into it. Mistakes are always going to happen. Watch any international test match and count the errors.

Teach your Outside-half to trust their ability and express themselves. Mistakes that happen on a pitch are a great way of testing the character of your players as individuals, but more importantly, they can help gauge how the team cohesively reacts to a mistake. Do your players lift others around them, or do they put others down when mistakes happen?

An Outside-half can expect both physical and mental pressure from the defence. Your players are looking for leadership and direction. An Outside-half needs to be able to handle the expectations while also putting their skills into practice.

Make training game realistic, practice how you would play. Pressure the Outside-half by creating environments that force them to make millisecond decisions and allow them to react to whatever the consequences may be. Flair is a gift that should not be kept hidden. Allow it to flourish, and you may well reap the rewards as both player and coach.

The best advice I can give to any Outside-half that wants to maximise their potential is simple. Practice your skills in pressure environments. Learn from the mistakes you make, but more importantly, be confident in your execution. There is no substitute for putting the hours in; communication is something that can only not be executed through fatigue or lack of want. Choose to be your best and enjoy what you do.

Role in defensive shapes and structures

In defence, the role of an Outside-half is to predominantly organise the defensive line and ensure the defensive system being used is executed.

The Outside-half should be looking to line up against their opposite player in defence.

If a team is operating an ABC system around the ruck, then the Outside-half will take up the position outside C, generally lining up against the opposition first receiver on the open side of the play.

When a tackle is performed, the Outside-half has a decision to make. The Outside-half will avoid competing for the ball in a ruck, and they will opt to remain in the defensive line, this allows them to organise the defence as well as be in a good position should a turn over occur.

Of course, if the ball is winnable at a ruck and the Outside-half is confident they can force a turnover, the Outside-half should enter the ruck and contest the ball. More often than not, the Outside-half will fold in defence; this means instead of contesting the ruck, they will get back in the line, folding to their designated position.

The same principle applies if the Outside-half hasn't made the tackle. They will still need to fold to the correct side and ensure they are lining up against the first receiver for the attacking team. In defence, the Outside-half should focus on getting in the line (organise), getting off the line (line speed), making the hit (stopping momentum) and getting on their feet (folding).

Of course, the skills mentioned here are ideals for the Outside-half when discussing their roles in the back line.

The best way to develop an Outside-half is to create environments through training or games that expose them to these situations and allow them to continue to work on their organisational roles within the team. The more time they have to practice their defensive position and attacking shape, the more effective they will be at leading their back line and the team around them.

Role in controlling different game scenarios

Game management is an aspect of the game that doesn't typically get discussed enough. We just expect our players to know what to do and how to do it. How often do we play a game of rugby, win, lose or draw, and then move on and prepare for next week's game? How often do we look back and think, what could we have done better? How can we improve this aspect of our game? A good Outside-half is someone that can manage the game. By this, what we are talking about, is managing how the game flows and runs. You are winning by two points with two minutes on the clock. What instructions are we giving? What do we want our Outside-half to be able to do? Look at American football or even soccer; clock management is a huge part of the game. As an Outside-half, we need to be smart.

Playing width-to-width rugby is fantastic if you are on top and winning possession easily. However, what do we do when this doesn't work? We need a plan B. A good Outside-half is one that can identify this and adapt to the game around them. We could write a whole book on this topic, so summarizing the subject on one page isn't doing it justice. However, we can try. To promote an understanding of game management is simple. Analyse your performance and identify what you could do to improve in certain situations. How often do you see a Outside-half kick from their 10m, miss touch, and the opposition immediately counter? Is this good game

50

management? You have released pressure for around five seconds and are now defending rather than attacking. Would a competitive box kick be a better option? Or perhaps keeping it in the forwards for another phase or two?

Of course, there are no easy answers, and as mentioned before, mistakes will happen. An Outside-half needs to know the game; they need to study and watch the excellent Outside-halves at the professional level. How do they kill the game? How do they generate forward momentum? How do they slow the game down to favor their own team's needs? There isn't one right answer. I suggest asking your Outside-half to compare and contrast their performance. What do they do that works and what could be better?

A great tactic when coaching is running team runs with more purpose. Give your team 10 seconds to form a lineout/scrum/restart and get the ball in play. We play a timer during games, why not training? Tell your players it's the last play of the game, they need a try to win. Any mistakes now will finish the game. The best thing about this is the Outside-half can control the players and dictate how the team plays. Practice as you play. If a habit is formed during training, there is more chance it will find its way into games.

Chapter 5:
Additional conditioning for the position of Outside-half

Overview

In this chapter you will gain knowledge of the following:

- ☑ **Conditioning for kicking**
- ☑ **Conditioning for passing**
- ☑ **Conditioning for open-field play**
- ☑ **Mental conditioning for the complete game**

Background

An Outside-half requires a certain level of conditioning to keep up with the flow of the game. They need to be able to pass exceptionally well, tackle, evade players, sprint past players and have the right cardiovascular endurance to remain influential for the full game. Handling, kicking, evasion, agility, and passing are all essential components to the modern day Outside-half.

Conditioning for kicking

There are many different types of kicks an Outside-half may have to perform during a match: grubbers, bombs, chips, box kicks, place kicks, etc. All of these types of kicks involve slightly different skills in terms of how the ball is held and at what point does the foot make contact with the ball.

If we however break these aspects of kicking down into the specific bio-mechanics of the kicking motion we can see that the force the player has to produce on the ball is actually not that great. The real secret to great kicking is about timing, coordination and the speed at which the foot makes contact with the ball i.e. foot speed.

Research has shown that the most significant determinant of kick power, outside of technique, is foot speed. That means the faster your foot is moving when it hits the ball, the higher your kicking range is likely to be, and the more accurate you can expect to be with your kicking over a given distance.

To increase the foot speed we need to understand where from within the body that speed is being generated. Large quad muscles and hamstrings aid in power, but not necessarily foot speed. The ability to generate foot speed comes from the abdomen and the abductor muscles that run from the inside of the thigh up and into the stomach. Within the modern gym there are many exercises for the legs, however there are almost none to develop foot speed.

One such exercise does however exist and we call this the high kick bungie.

To perform this exercise you first wrap a bungie band around a solid object such as a squat rack. Next you wrap the other end of the bungie around the non-kicking foot and move it as high up the thigh as it can go. Next you place the non-kicking foot on a raised platform for height elevation.

Because the load involved in kicking is small and the movement speed is high, you don't need to use a significant amount of load when training to improve kicking power.

This drill shares a near identical range of movement, movement speed, and contraction type as a real kick, which should ensure a high degree of transfer from this training exercise to the field.

Conditioning for passing

The passing action is reasonably easy to develop if the correct technique is used. To be great at passing the secret is to be able to generate a lot of rotational force at high-speed while coordinating the upper and lower body together. Depending on how you pass, the force contribution of the lower body can go up or down, but the torso and upper body are the primary drivers of the passing action.

This exercise is called wall slams and is a great way to develop both passing skill and passing power

Set up this drill with a 3-5kg medicine ball in an athletic stance at 90 degrees to the wall. Wind up by dropping your weight into your far leg, dipping at your hip, knee, and ankle, and rotating your torso away from the wall. Then quickly reverse the direction, extending powerfully at your hip, knee, and ankle, turn your torso to the wall, and follow through by exploding with your arms. The most potent throw will come when you transfer force up from the lower body to the upper body like a wave.

Aim for 6-10 reps per side for 3-5 sets with full rest periods of 3-4 minutes each between sets.

Conditioning for open field play

Attacking is a crucial part of the game. Evasion, agility, power, and speed are all skills that enable an Outside-half to penetrate a defensive line of attack. Speed endurance allows an Outside-half to maintain their speed over 20-30m. By training these areas, an Outside-half will see benefits to the physical aspects of their game.

- **Agility ladder** -
  The agility
  ladder is an
  impressive bit of
  kit that allows
  athletes to work
  on their speed
  and agility.
  There are many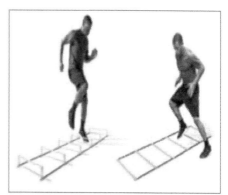
  methods when practicing your footwork. Focus
  on the fundamentals, good posture, light feet,
  opposite arm to opposite leg and a beautiful
  drive with your running motion.

- **Sled Sprint** -
  Start with a
  three-point
  stance. The
  first few steps
  should be
  short and
  sharp, keeping
  the center of gravity low, slowly increasing
  height and leg drive. Push through your sprint
  with nice arm and leg drive.

- **Barbell twists** - Feet should be shoulder width apart. Arms remain straight and locked out, then twist the barbell from a sideways position (left to right).

Mental conditioning for the complete game

Playing Outside-half comes with a lot of pressure. You are required to make continuous decisions to help better your team's chances of winning.

Of course, not all of these will come off. However, since an Outside-half will make hundreds of decisions during a game, it is essential that the developing player practices decision-making under pressure and also learns how to deal with mistakes. Below are some suggestions to help work on mental conditioning.

- **Make training specific and game realistic** - Practice as you play. As a player, always ask yourself, is this drill game particular, how can we add pressure? Using a defender in drills is often a good idea.

- **Watch your own game -** Are the decisions you make in matches the best ones? If not, how can you change your game to rectify this?
- **Watch other Outside-halves** - At the top level and see how they react to different situations. Look at what their team needs from them and how they manage to meet their teammate's needs.
- **Play other evasive sports** – Soccer is a great example, not only will it imporve your kicking skills, it evasive nature will help you learn how to work space as well as identify how space can be created by working off the ball.
- **Reaching your limit.** - You need to learn just what your body is capable of achieving. Often it is the mind that stops us from physically reaching our maximum.
- **Dare to flair.** - You are an Outside-half. Your job is to be the role model for your teammates. Use your skills at the right time.

Chapter 6:
The essential knowledge for developing great rugby

Overview

In this chapter you will gain knowledge of the following:

- ☑ **Young player development**
- ☑ **Catch and pass skills development**
- ☑ **Tackling skills development**
- ☑ **Breakdown skills development**

Young player development

Children go through predictable growth periods known as developmental milestones. These milestones are broken into main areas of development.

- **Cognitive Development** - This is the child's ability to learn and solve problems. For example, this includes a two-month-old baby learning to explore the environment with hands or eyes.
- **Social and Emotional Development** - This is the child's ability to interact with others, including helping themselves and self-control. Examples of this type of development would include a boy knowing how to take turns in games at school.

- **Fine Motor Skill Development** - This is the child's ability to use small muscles, specifically their hands and fingers, to pick up small objects, hold a spoon, turn pages in a book, or use a crayon to draw.
- **Speech and Language Development** - This is the child's ability to both understand and use language. For example, this includes a 12-month-old baby saying his first words and a two-year-old naming parts of his body.

Why is it important to know these things if we are developing rugby players? Well, if we know how a young player develops from ages six into adulthood, we can adjust our speech, words, drills, and attitude to ensuring that players have a positive experience in the sport of rugby union.

Catch and pass skills development

To become competent in the sport of rugby union, a developing player needs to learn how to catch and pass the ball at a proficient level and to work within the team environment. To do this effectively the developing player needs to learn five types of basic passing.

1. **Basic pass** - This is a very versatile pass that can be used in many situations. It allows you to easily control the speed and distance of the pass.

2. **Long clearing pass** - This pass is used most often when you are the Scrum-half or the player acting in that role. You remove the ball from the base of the scrum or a ruck and send it out to the backs. If you position your feet and arms well in relation to the ball, you can pass swiftly, giving the receiver more time and space.

3. **Close support pass** - You use two hands for this pass; gentle and soft to close players. Move your arms to disguise what you are doing, but supply power mainly with your fingers, giving great control over short distances.

4. **Get out of trouble pass** - Useful when a long ground pass is required but you are not in the correct position to make one and are being pressured which prevents you from taking time to get set. A risky pass. Should only be attempted by the highly skilled in dire emergencies.

5. **Over head pass** - You use this pass to get the ball to a supporting player when there is an opposition player directly between you and your support. The lobbing motion allows the ball to travel in an arc above and out of reach of your opponent(s).

Tackling skills development

Tackling is one of the absolute fundamentals of rugby and as such needs to be learned, re-enforced and continuously worked upon during a player's career. If the technique is learned safely and thoroughly at an early age, then that player will always be able to execute the skill and take joy from that part of the game.

Front on tackle (passive)

This tackle is commonly referred to as the sacrifice tackle. If perfected, it will be achieved every time, regardless of the opponent's size, height, and strength.

To successfully execute this technique the following process is followed

- Imagine the target on the bottom of the ball carrier's shorts.
- When tackling, keep the head up and with the chin of the chest.
- Brace the shoulders.
- Make initial contact with shoulders on the ball carrier's thigh.
- Keep the arms around the carrier's legs.

- Keep the head up and to one side of the ball carrier's legs.
- Use momentum to take the ball carrier over the shoulder.
- Twist around and land on top of the tackled player.
- Get up immediately after the tackle and compete for the ball.
- The child's ability to use small muscles, specifically their hands and fingers, to pick up small objects, hold a spoon, turn pages in a book, or use a crayon to draw.

Front on tackle (active)

The objective of this tackle is to drive the ball carrier behind the advantage line. To successfully execute this technique the following process is followed:

- Get the lead foot as close as possible to the ball carrier.
- Keep eyes on the point of contact.
- Keep head to one side.
- Drop hips to lower the centre of gravity.
- Drive shoulder up to the centre of the target either into the stomach or onto the chest.
- Power comes from an explosive drive upwards emanating from the legs and buttocks.
- Wrap the arms around the player.

- If possible pick one leg up.
- Keep driving until the attacking player's balance is broken and you are in control of his body.
- Continue forward landing onto of the attacking player.
- Get up immediately after the tackle and compete for the ball.

Side on tackle

This kind of tackle requires the tackler to anticipate the future point of contact and then track the ball carrier. Once the tackler has positioned the ball carrier into the desired position, then the following process should be followed:

- Get the lead foot as close as possible to the ball carrier.
- Imagine the target on the bottom of the ball carrier's shorts.
- When tackling, keep the head up and with the chin of the chest.
- Brace the shoulders.
- Make initial contact with shoulders on the ball carrier's thigh.
- Keep the arms around the carrier's legs.
- Keep the head up and to one side of the ball carrier's legs.

- Use momentum to take the ball carrier over the shoulder.
- Twist around and land on top of the tackled player.
- Get up immediately after the tackle and compete for the ball.

Rear tackle

This tackle requires the tackler to anticipate the future point of contact and possess an attitude that means he never gives up. A rear tackle is normally used when an attacker has broken the gain line and is heading for the try line. It's not so much about ability, it's about attitude and commitment. Once the tackler has got close enough to the ball carrier, then the following process should be followed:

- Get the lead foot as close as possible to the ball carrier.
- Imagine the target on the bottom of the ball carrier's shorts.
- When tackling keep the head up and with the chin of the chest.
- Brace the shoulders.
- Make initial contact with shoulders on the ball carrier's thigh.

- Keep the arms around the carrier's legs.
- Keep the head up and to one side of the ball carrier's legs.
- Drive with the legs, gripping with arms and hands to bring the ball carrier to the ground.
- Land on top of the tackled player.
- Get up immediately after the tackle and compete for the ball.

Smother tackle

The idea of the smother tackle is to wrap the ball carrier up so that he can neither pass the ball nor release the ball. This kind of tackle should be taught to players who are already proficient in the other forms of tackling rather than use it as the primary tackle technique. To successfully execute this technique the following process is followed:

- Get the lead foot as close as possible to the ball carrier.
- Keep eyes on the point of contact.
- Wrap the arms around the upper part of the ball carrier's body.
- Trap the ball and the player's arms.
- Add your own weight to the ball carrier and bring the player to the ground.
- Land on top of the tackled player.

Breakdown skills development

A breakdown happens when there is a stop in the forward momentum but the ball is still live and in active play. The three scenarios where this happens are as follows:

- **Tackle** - Only the ball carrier can be tackled by an opposing player. A tackle occurs when the ball carrier is held by one or more opponents and is brought to the ground, i.e. has one or both knees on the ground, is sitting on the ground or is on top of another player who is on the ground. To maintain the continuity of the game, the ball carrier must release the ball immediately after the tackle, the tackler must release the ball carrier and both players must roll away from the ball. This allows other players to come in and contest for the ball, thereby starting a new phase of play.

• **Ruck -** A ruck is formed if the ball is on the ground and one or more players from each team are on their feet close around it. Players must not handle the ball in the ruck, and must use their feet to move the ball or drive over it so that it emerges at the team's hindmost foot, at which point it can be picked up.

- **Maul** – When the ball carrier is held, but not brought to the ground, a maul may be formed. For a maul to form there must be at least three players involved, including the ball carrier, an opponent holding the ball carrier, and a team mate of the ball carrier bound to the ball carrier. When a maul has formed, it must keep moving forward towards a goal-line. The players must stay on their feet. Once a maul has been formed, an offside line comes into force for both teams which is parallel to the goal-line and right behind the foot of the hindmost player in the maul.

By understanding the concepts and rules surrounding the breakdown, we can look to coach the skills that are most effective during this critical part of the game.

Chapter 7:
Understanding the body for developing players

Overview

In this chapter you will gain knowledge of the following:

- ☑ **How the body works**
- ☑ **How the body grows**
- ☑ **Common injuries and prevention strategies**

Background

There is a whole science behind how the body works; specifically there is a whole industry that supports the training, recovery and development of rugby players.

A fundamental understanding of the body's energy system, and how it grows after exercise, will greatly assist the player in his understanding, and therefore inform him on selecting supplements to support his development if he wishes.

How the body works

If you are a scientist, or an expert in nutrition, you may understand the difference between Non-oxidative

(Anaerobic) and Oxidative (Aerobic) systems, but what do these terms really mean?

Non-oxidative (without oxygen) supplies rely on using stored resources known as adenosine triphosphate (ATP), phosphocreatine (PC), and the production of lactic acid (LA) and do not go into using oxygen to produce more energy. With oxidative (with oxygen), the body uses oxygen to aid in energy production through what is called the Krebs cycle. This whole process is called oxidation phosphorylation. The standard energy of all human motion is the release of energy. Therefore, replenishment of ATP or the removal and/or dissipation of the waste products associated with maintaining our ATP supplies are what happens inside our bodies when we play sports.

A trained rugby player knows how the system works and, as such, knows how to replenish the ATP that is being used. The three major components: ATP/PC, LA and oxidative have the ability to support activities of varying intensities and durations.

All athletes have the ability to produce power and work intensities that exceed their ability to resynthesize ATP. For example, even in a 100m sprint on the track, the athlete slows down due to fatigue. Similarly, in a series of five lineout jumps or explosive scrums, power output drops.

The stages of energy usage in the body

Physiologists have devised a method to look at the energy expenditures of different sports.

The first phase is called the ATP- PC system. ATP (Adenosine Triphosphate) is stored in all cells, particularly muscles. In a sense, it is free energy because the body stores ATP to make it available for immediate use, however, you can only use it once and it needs recovery time to restore. The ATP system is great for short and quick activities because it only lasts for about five seconds and is used in activities like 10-meter sprints.

When ATP is used it breaks down into adenosine diphosphate (ADP). ADP then can combine with phosphocreatine (PC) to make more ATP, but only for a short period of time, around 5-20 seconds. This system requires some recovery time as well. It takes about 25-30 seconds to regain about half of the phosphocreatine stores. These two systems combine for activities like 200m sprints and sports where short intermittent bursts of activity are required, for example, basketball, hockey, and rugby.

The next major phase is called the lactic (LA) system. After the 20 seconds of the ATP-PC system, the body requires another ingredient, muscle glycogen (glucose) to be added to continue.

This system begins when phosphocreatine stores are depleted. Lactic acid (or lactate) comes from the breakdown of the glucose released from the muscles. One of the outcomes of this breakdown is that positive Hydrogen ions are expelled which accumulate in the muscles and causes them to fatigue.

The lactic system is used in a number of sports that do repeat sprinting or high-energy activities, such as rugby, sprint cycling, 100m swim, and 400 meter sprints in athletics.

Training can therefore be designed to help the rugby player improve their tolerance to the buildup of the positive hydrogen ions. Training sessions of intense training, lasting from 25 to 45 seconds, with rest ranging from 20 seconds to three minutes.

The third system is the Oxidative phase. In this phase, as the term indicates, you are using oxygen to fuel the breakdown of carbohydrates first, free fatty acids second and if the exercise continues long enough - protein. Whereas, the previous systems have related to higher intensity work (or power) the aerobic system is more of moderate or low-intensity work, but of longer duration.

The oxidative system should be developed to aid in the lactic system. The development of the aerobic system aids in lactate removal, so that the athlete can tolerate more lactate. Training to develop this system consists of the traditional long runs, but can also have repeats of shorter distances of low intensity with reduced rest (20 x 200m with 30-second rest).

How the body grows

When we talk about training it can be simplified to three stages: stress, recovery, and adaptation. As a player, the challenge is to work the body (stress) through training, take a period of recovery (rest) and then allow the improvement to happen (adaption).

- **Stress** – Getting the body to work.
- **Recovery** – Letting the body recover.
- **Adaption** – Enabling the body to grow.

Through adaptation, the rugby player can gradually develop the capability to handle more training or training with more intensity. As a player, you need to manipulate combinations of training frequency (how often you train), training intensity (how hard you train), and training duration (how long you train).

Another key factor is how the training you are doing relates to your playing standard and position. Physiologists call this Specific Adaptations to Imposed Demands (SAID).

Stress stage

Chapter 3 of this book contains a number of exercises designed to specifically stress the body of a rugby player. Chapter 5 of this book identifies the specific exercise for this specific playing position on the rugby field. Use these exercises and the knowledge of the ATP-CP energy system to design your own specific workout that will help you develop as a rugby player.

Rest stage

Essentially the rest stage should start with warming down of the body using the same exercises prior to the stress stage.

Next comes rehydration. This depends on your sweat rate, but on average, a player will cover between 8 and 12 kilometers a game. To work out how much you need to drink to rehydrate it is best to weigh yourself before and after training. If you lose 1.5 kg in sweat you should replace 1.2-1.5 times that amount. That means slowly consuming between 1.8 to 2.25 liters of fluid at the end of each training session or match.

Adaptation stage

In response to any form of movement, the body undergoes a multitude of adaptations, both acute (sudden, temporary changes in body function caused by physical exertion are termed acute), and chronic (adaptations that enable the body to respond more favourably to subsequent training sessions). The four key adaptions that enable athletes to perform better are the lungs, heart, muscles and, bones.

- **The lungs** - The lungs become more adept at ventilating larger volumes of air during intense physical exertion.
- **The heart** - The main heart adaptation is an increase in size, as it works to accommodate a greater cardiac output from session to session.
- **The muscles** - An aerobically trained muscle has more capillaries and mitochondria leading to a greater capacity to store fuel.
- **The bones** - The skeletal system involves the process of re-modelling (when cells called osteoclasts break down old bone as cells called osteoblasts replace it with new tissue to make it denser and stronger).

Common injuries and prevention strategies

Rugby players wear very little, if any, protective equipment, and their body is exposed to all of those hard hits. Studies have shown that injuries are the most common reason for players to quit playing rugby. Successive injuries over time can lead to long-term effects. Injuries common to rugby include muscle strains, knee sprains, contusions, hip dislocations, and facial injury.

Most Common Rugby Injuries

There are many injuries that can take place during the course of a game, the most common ones are identified below:

- **Muscle Strain** - When competing in rugby or practicing for competition, the muscles are stressed and stretched repeatedly. A hard-driving scrum or a move to evade a defender can place the muscles at risk of tearing. When the muscle tears it becomes weaker, pain and tenderness set in, and some slight swelling and bruising may occur. A minor strain will respond to ice, rest, and allow a return to full activity within one to two weeks.

- **Knee Sprain** - Any of the ligaments in the knee are subject to sprain in a hard-hitting rugby game. The most common sprains include the anterior cruciate ligament (ACL) and the medial collateral ligament (MCL.) The ACL is often torn when the foot and lower leg are planted, but the upper leg rotates. The MCL is commonly sprained by contact from another player on the outside of the knee. The severity of the sprain is determined by the amount of tearing present in the ligament, with the worst being a complete rupture. Minor sprains may take two to three weeks for recovery, while a total tear may take eight weeks. Ice, and immobilization will help with recovery.

- **Bruises and Contusions** - As with any contact sport, bruises and contusions are very common in rugby. Players are being impacted in many directions, and those hard-hits result in blood vessels under the skin rupturing which causes swelling, pain, discoloration, and tenderness. Most contusions can be treated with ice. Deeper contusions in the muscle tissue may require rest and a gradual return to

Injury prevention strategies

To compete in the modern game of rugby a rugby player should develop a natural protective layering (musculature) and be strong enough to withstand the physical impacts of the game.

Practicing the game and becoming proficient in the skills of rugby condition the body when delivering a tackle, or taking one, which will help the player avoid some of the most common injuries in rugby.

Use of the minimal protective equipment such as a mouth guard would help shield the body from some of the usual injuries encountered in a game or during practice.

Strength training will help build protective muscle tissue over the bones and joints and will help keep the body healthy for games and speed recovery should an injury occur.

Flexibility is vital to condition the body to cope when it is twisted and contorted at different angles during tackles or when avoiding a defender, so a good flexibility routine is essential.

The top three rugby stretches

Stretching is one of the most under-utilized techniques for improving athletic performance, preventing sports injury, and properly rehabilitating sprain and strain injury. Don't make the mistake of thinking that something as simple as stretching won't be useful. The following three essential stretching exercises are very beneficial for rugby players.

- **Reaching-up shoulder stretch** - Place one hand behind your back and then reach up between your shoulder blades.

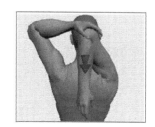

- **Lying knee roll-over stretch** - While lying on your back, bend your knees and let them fall to one side. Keep your arms out to the side and let your back and hips rotate with your knees.

- **Kneeling Quad Stretch** - Kneel on one foot and the other knee. If needed, hold on to something to keep your balance and then push your hips forward.

Chapter 8:
Natural windows for player development

Overview

In this chapter you will gain knowledge of the following:

☑ **Development windows**
☑ **Anatomical adaption**

Background

Developing players, who are committed to their own success, continually look to improve themselves. Whether it be developing their attacking, defensive, physical or mental conditioning, or working on the core essentials of positional specific excellence, they desire to be the very best they can be.

As humans, we are continually learning and developing new skills through life experiences. There are, however, some extraordinary development windows during the younger years of five to seventeen whereby the developing rugby player can accelerate the skills needed for exceptional rugby.

Development windows

Strength and conditioning is an absolutely essential part of developing a competent player in the sport of rugby union.

However, to progress, the player, family, coach and support network must understand the 'windows' of development within the young athlete.

- **Skills window** – This occurs between the approximate ages of 8 to 11 for girls and 9 to 12 years of age for boys.
- **Speed window** - During the growth spurt for boys it is important for coaches to understand the Long Term Player Development Pathway (FTPDP) if they are to successfully take advantage of opportunities for skill and fitness development and maintain the players commitment to the sport they love.

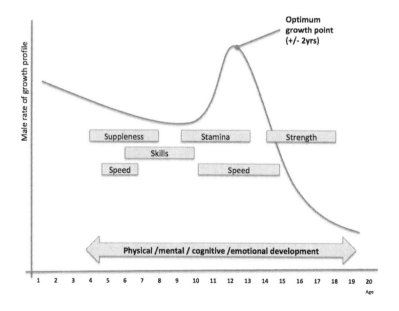

There is ample evidence showing that children and teenagers can improve in strength (Falk and Tenembaum, 1996, Payne et al., 1997), anaerobic fitness (Tolfrey, 2007) and aerobic fitness (Baquet et al., 2003) as well as speed, balance and stability (Gilligan et al., 2005). Further, resistance training, when completed under the qualified supervision of an adult, is safe, and gains can be made by children as young as 8 to 10 years of age (Payne et al., 1997, Falk and Tenembaum, 1996).

Given the possibilities for improved general fitness within developing players, it is important not to assume that scaled-down adult program are appropriate.

The process of growth and development, which occurs throughout the pre-teenage and teenage years, needs to be understood so that appropriate development of a player is managed in a safe, progressive and enjoyable manner.

Long Term Player Development Pathway (LTPDP)

As regards the adult game, we are aware of the importance of ensuring that the player is developed and prepared to play in a periodised and progressive manner. The latter stages of the Long Term Player Development Pathway (LTPDP), including the "Learn to Compete" and "Train to Win" stages, provide guidelines for the strength and conditioning coach at the adult game level.

Functional screening is an effective method of observing movement imbalances within a player during the "Training to Train" and "Training to Compete "windows which, if corrected early, can improve the player's enjoyment within the game and increase the duration they can remain in the "Training to Win" phase.

85

Chapter 9:
Recognition pathways for developing players

Overview

In this chapter you will gain knowledge of the following:

☑ **Player development pathways**
☑ **Competency framework**

Player development pathways

There are many ways for a young rugby player to be recognised at an elite level, and official pathways do exist to help identify and develop those players at club and regional levels.

Whereas it is fully understood that different kids develop at different ages, it is beneficial for the young athlete to understand the pathways early so they can get access to the higher levels of coaching needed and to get on the "rugby radar".

Those "rugby radars" can be very subjective, especially at the early stages of development, and that is why the core disciplines of catch and pass, tackling, and breakdown skills need to be continuously developed and honed through those development years.

Australian Rugby Union development pathway

This is the current publicised pathways for developing rugby players in Australia (2017).

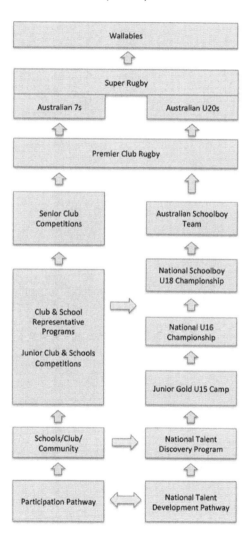

New Zealand 15 aside development pathway

This is the current publicised junior pathways for developing rugby players in New Zealand (2017).

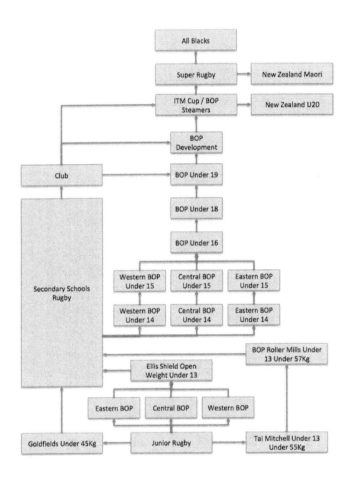

USA Rugby development pathway

This is the current publicised junior pathways for developing rugby players in America (2017).

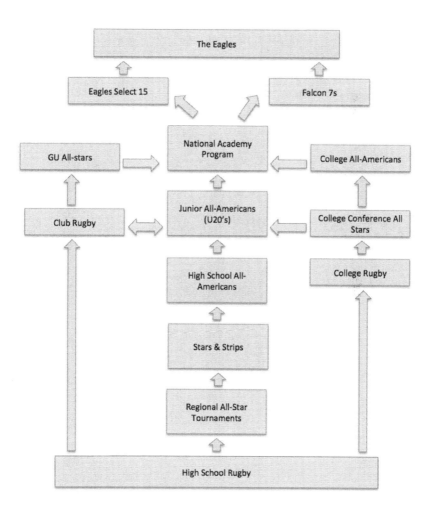

English Rugby Union development pathway

This is the current publicised junior pathways for developing rugby players in England (2017).

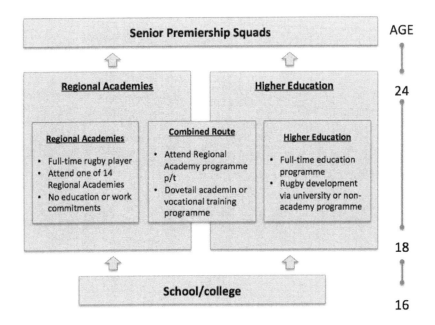

Welsh Rugby Union development pathway

This is the current publicised junior pathways for developing rugby players in Wales (2017).

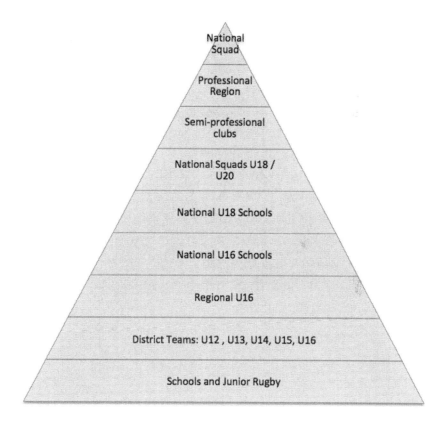

Competency framework

Many players, coaches and supportive family members spend a lot of time and effort trying to identify their development route to becoming a professional rugby player. Some will even go as far as to change region, jobs and even countries in pursuit of development paths that meet their needs. Sometimes getting recognised by the right development officer or national scout is a matter of luck and timing, however that just gets you started.

Develop A Player has developed a free professional player profile at www.developaplayer.com where players can record and promote their rugby successes. Additionally all developing players from ages six through to seniors can get access and record their competency development at each age and against each position thereby allowing them to become the architect of their own development success.

Attacking competency framework

Skill	Description	Level 1	Level 2	Level 3
Scrum	Scrummaging ability in specific position.	Understands role on the pitch in attack.	Performs well at set pieces to disrupt opposition.	Leads set pieces and is effective at disrupting opposition ball.
Lineout	Lineout ability in specific position.	Understands role on the pitch in attack.	Performs well at set pieces and in broken play.	Leads lineouts and is effective at attacking plays.
Restarts	Ability to be effective in restarts.	Understands restart concepts of attack.	Can read restart positioning and adapts.	Mastery in restart situations.
Breakdown	Ability to be effective at the breakdown.	Understands the basics of the breakdown.	Contributes at the breakdown and is effective.	Expert at the breakdown in attack.

Open Play	Ability to attack in open play.	Understands the basics of attack.	Effective in attack with the ball.	Effective in attack with or without the ball.
Catch and Pass	Ability to catch and pass the ball.	Can catch and pass the ball.	Effective in catch and pass.	Effective in all types of catch and pass.
Kicking	Ability to kick.	Can kick the ball effectively.	Effective in all aspects of kicking attack.	Mastery in kicking ability in attack.
Shapes and Structures	Attacking shapes and structures.	Understands basic shapes and structures.	Understands where to use shapes and structures.	Can adapt shapes and structures to game situations.

		Understands different parts of the field	Understand parts of the field and what plays to use.	Mastery in field movement and appropriate plays
Field Positioning	**Understands Field segmentation.**			
Rules of the Game	**Understanding of the rules.**	Understands the basic rules of the game.	Understands the advanced rules of the game.	Has a deep understanding of the rules of the game.

Defensive competency framework

Skill	Description	Level 1	Level 2	Level 3
Scrum	Scrummaging ability in specific position.	Understands role when the opposition has the ball.	Understands role when the opposition has the ball and can have an impact	Leads set pieces and has an impact on the opposition
Lineout	Lineout ability in specific position.	Understands role when the opposition has the ball.	Understands role when the opposition has the ball and can have an impact	Leads the lineout and has an impact on the opposition
Restarts	Ability to be effective in restarts.	Understands restart concepts of defence.	Can read restart positioning and adapts.	Mastery in restart situations.

Breakdown	**Ability to be effective at the breakdown.**	Understands the basics of the breakdown.	Contributes at the breakdown in defence	Expert at the breakdown and can force turn-overs
Open Play	**Ability to attack in open play.**	Understands the basics of defence in open play.	Effective in open play defence.	Effective in open play defence and has an impact on the oppositions attack capability
Kicking	**Ability to kick.**	Understands different parts of the field while in defence	Understands defensive policies in defending kicks.	Mastery in field defence and adapts to opposition kicks.
Shapes and Structures	**Attacking shapes and structures.**	Understands the basic rules of defensive shapes and structures	Understands the defensive shapes and structures and can adapt	Has a deep understanding of defensive shapes and structures and can influence the attacking options.

		Understands role on the pitch in defence.	Understands and anticipates field positioning in defence	Understands, adapts and has an impact of the attacking ability of a team by defensive field positioning.
Field Positioning	**Understands Field segmentation.**	Understands role on the pitch in defence.	Understands and anticipates field positioning in defence	Understands, adapts and has an impact of the attacking ability of a team by defensive field positioning.
Rules of the Game	**Understanding of the rules.**	Understands role on the pitch in defence.	Has a good understanding of all the defensive rules of the game.	Has a deep understanding of the defensive rules of the game

Physical conditioning competency framework

Skill	Description	Level 1	Level 2	Level 3
Scrum	Scrummaging conditioning in specific position.	Has the core conditioning to perform in the role.	Has developed good conditioning to perform well in the role.	Has developed advanced conditioning to perform exceptionally in the role.
Lineout	Lineout conditioning in specific position.	Has the core conditioning to perform in the role.	Has developed good conditioning to perform well in the role.	Has developed advanced conditioning to perform exceptionally in the role.
Breakdown	Conditioning to be effective at the breakdown.	Has the core conditioning to be effective at the breakdown.	Has the core conditioning to impact the breakdown.	Has the core conditioning to significantly impact the breakdown

		Has the core conditioning to perform in open play.	Has the conditioning to be effective in open play.	Has developed advanced conditioning for open play rugby.
Open Play	**Conditioning for open play.**			
Catch and Pass	**Conditioning for catch and pass.**	Has the core conditioning to effectively catch and pass.	Has the conditioning to be effective in catch and pass.	Has developed advanced conditioning for catch and pass skills.

Mental conditioning competency framework

Skill	Description	Level 1	Level 2	Level 3
Set piece	Mental conditioning for set piece rugby.	Has the core mental conditioning for set piece rugby.	Has developed good mental conditioning for set piece rugby.	Has developed advanced mental conditioning for set piece rugby.
Catch and Pass	Mental conditioning Catch and Pass.	Has the core mental conditioning to perform catch and pass	Has developed good mental conditioning for advanced catch and pass.	Has developed advanced mental conditioning for excellent catch and pass skills under pressure
Breakdown	Mental conditioning for breakdown.	Has the core mental conditioning to perform at the breakdown.	Has developed good mental conditioning to perform at the breakdown.	Has developed advanced mental conditioning to perform at the breakdown.
Open Play	Mental conditioning for open play.	Has the core mental conditioning to perform in the role.	Has the mental conditioning to be effective in open play.	Has developed advanced mental conditioning for open play.

101

Courage to Win	Mental conditioning to win.	Understands mental visualization.	Can utilise effective mental imagery.	Mastery at effective mental imagery.

Chapter 10:
Develop A Player developmental portal

Overview

In this chapter you will gain knowledge of the following:

☑ **Our purpose**
☑ **Free professional player profile for Outside-half (No.10)**

Our purpose

Develop A Player was established with a specific purpose, which was to remove the participation barrier for all players wanting to take part in the sport of rugby union.

To set up your FREE Professional Player Profile you just need to go to: **www.developaplayer.com**

Free professional player profile for a Outside-half

- **Step 1** – Click on Player Zone Registration to get this screen.
- **Step 2** – Enter a valid e-mail address and create a password.
- **Step 3** – Enter your name, Date of Birth and nationality.
- **Step 4** – Upload a profile picture (.jpeg).
- **Step 5** – Enter your player information.
- **Step 6** – Read and accept the terms and conditions and privacy policy.
- **Step 7** – Click register.

You will receive a one-time password in your e-mail inbox. Enter that code into the confirmation screen and then you're all done.

Welcome to Develop A Player.

References and acknowledgements

Balyi and Way, 2005

Falk and Tenembaum, 1996, Payne et al. 1997

Tolfrey, 2007

Baquet et al. 2003

Gilligan et al. 2005.

Payne et al. 1997, Falk and Tenembaum, 1996.

Develop A Player, 2012

ARU, 2015

www.developaplayer.com

Printed in Great Britain
by Amazon

28973641R00064